CHOOSING FORGIVENESS

Trusting God
to see us through the tragedy
of our daughter's murder

Paul Marshall

Printed in the United States of America
ISBN 978-1-946425-14-0

Book Design by CSinclaire Write-Design
Cover Design by Klevur

WRITEWAY
PUBLISHING

CHOOSING FORGIVENESS

With appreciation to
Jeanan Jackson
for her diligence and dedication in
helping me create this book
and
Jeff Cregg
for the help he has provided
to allow me to spread the message
found in this book.

Both have been instrumental in the
telling of Wende's story.

PROLOGUE

CHOOSING FORGIVENESS
nurtured by faith, family, and friends

I love you, too, Dad!

I RECEIVED A SURPRISE call from our daughter Wende one late October morning in 2013. She told me she had picked up some nails in her tires and two of them were flat. She explained that a neighbor was having their roof replaced and the nails likely came from that work. She said she probably wouldn't be able to go to work because of the flat tires. Wende was working as a Contracts Administrator at Air Liquide, an industrial gas service company. Her position was temporary, but she expected to be made permanent within a couple of weeks. It was a great opportunity with a decent salary and a bright future. Because it was important for her to get to work that day, I volunteered to assist in changing and repairing her tires. Then she told me that a former boyfriend named Colt Morgan was there with her and would fix the tires, but not in time to get her to work.

It was my understanding that Colt had recently been in jail for 90 days for a DWI. We didn't know he had reconnected with Wende. I was uneasy because we had tried to learn more about Colt prior to his arrest, and he'd never been willing to meet with us. We'd made several attempts to get him to join in the Marshall family gatherings, but he was never available. So it came as quite a surprise when she announced in this phone call that he had proposed marriage. I asked to speak to Colt and told him he was making a wise decision. Then I ended my phone conversation with Wende on the line.

"I love you, Wende."

"I love you, too, Dad."

That was the last thing she ever said to me.

ONE

I've got to tell you something that's not easy to say.
DETECTIVE MICHAEL RITCHIE, HARRIS COUNTY SHERIFF'S OFFICE

COLT WAS AN UNKNOWN to us. He seemed quite different from any of Wende's past boyfriends. Her past partners were usually outgoing, gregarious, and full of humor. Colt was remote, distant, and quite unsure of himself. I had an uncomfortable feeling, knowing Wende as I did, that she wanted to fix him. They'd only known each other about a year, having met while both were working at a production company called Norriseal. Because of this, Wende's announcement of her engagement to Colt made us uneasy.

We wanted to know Colt better and to discuss their marriage plans so we arranged to meet for dinner with her and Colt on the coming Friday, the first of November. We knew that Colt did not have a job and did not appear to be actively looking for one. That was a dangerous situation on which to start a marriage. He was 28 years old, and Wende was taking care of him. It was almost like she'd adopted him as she had her two rescue dogs. Because Wende had just celebrated her forty-fourth birthday earlier that month, we also wanted to discuss their plans for children.

My wife, GG, spoke with Wende on Wednesday to confirm the Friday dinner. We were very excited to learn more about their future plans. Friday came. No Wende. No Colt. We called both her cell phone and her home number. We texted her. Where were they? My guess—they had eloped.

On Saturday I drove to Wende's house to check on her. I had the wrong key. I called her best friend, Jennifer, and learned Wende had failed to show up on Thursday although she had planned to go trick-or-treating that Halloween night with Jennifer and her daughter. We agreed to meet Jennifer and John, Jenn's fiancé, Sunday morning after church at Wende's place. All four of us knew something was very wrong as soon as we entered the house.

Wende's house.

Her two adopted dogs, Tori and Terra, were alone without food or water. Wende would never have done anything that cruel to those dogs. Once she took a dog from a homeless man while stopped at a traffic light. He said she looked like an animal lover, and he could no longer care for his dog. Wende was between jobs at the time and on a limited budget. Yet she took the dog and spent several hundred dollars to have it spayed, vaccinated, and checked for general health problems.

Tori and Terra appeared very disturbed and anxious. That they were left unattended was a major clue that things were not right. They were like children to Wende.

We found Wende's clothes neatly laid out for work. Her car, cell phone, and purse were still at her home. We also found a strange note from Colt in her purse.

"*I hope you are ok. I hate it when you get drunk like that and leave,*" he wrote. But why would she have left without her phone or purse?

He apologized for not getting the hallway painted. "*I started painting like you asked, but the color that matches is all dried up.*"

The note made it clear he thought that right now they should not be together.

"*You are a good person Wende, but I don't think we are the best for each other. I need to stand on my own 2 feet before I should consider marriage. I am going to San Antonio to see my brother. Then head out to El Paso. I've been given an opportunity for employoment [sic] there.*"

He forgave her for their argument and asked for her

forgiveness as well. ". . . *if you consider moving to El Paso maybe we'll work out and get married.*"[1]

Why would Wende leave without her phone? Did she go with a friend? Her car was still at the house. It didn't make any sense to us. There was a hole in the sheetrock of the master bedroom, and all the trash cans looked recently cleaned as did the fireplace.

I looked on Wende's cell phone for recent calls. The first number was to someone named Michael. I hit redial and when Michael answered, I asked him when he'd spoken with Wende.

He said, "I didn't speak with Wende. I spoke to Colt. He wanted a ride from his girlfriend's house to his car."

I said to him, "This is Wende's dad. She's disappeared. Your number is the last one called on her phone."

Michael sounded concerned when he said, "Colt was acting very strange when I picked him up on Thursday afternoon around four. Said he'd had a heated argument with Wende, and she went off with a friend. And he had this ugly cut on his hand. Told me he did this while opening a package of hot dogs.[2] I drove him to my house, and my wife dressed the wound. We tried to get him to go to the hospital to have it stitched, but Colt refused. She fixed him a sandwich and then insisted we take him to his car. She was uncomfortable with him around. Sir, you need to call the cops."

I called the Harris County Precinct 4 Constables' Office to file a missing person's report. At around four p.m. on

Sunday, the third of November, Deputy Joel Burke came to our home to take our statement.

"A forty-four-year-old unmarried woman is not going to get much attention given the volume of work most agencies have on a day-to-day basis," he said after getting all of our information. But Burke called me later that evening and suggested I meet him at Wende's house for a welfare check. He needed my permission to enter but said I didn't need to stick around and that he would lock up afterwards and return the key to me.

That same evening, with our daughter Michele and son-in-law Andrew present, I made additional calls from Wende's recent call list. Among them were Colt's mother, Teresa, and his brother. She told me Colt's grandmother noticed him acting strangely when he visited her on Friday night. Colt told her Wende had called off the engagement. Teresa gave me some more numbers where he might be reached.

From the numbers they gave us, we came in contact with a friend of Colt's in Palestine, Texas. Colt was there with him. I asked Colt if he knew where Wende was. He said the last time he saw her was around nine or ten p.m. on Halloween at her house. He assured us there was no physical violence.

"We had an argument. She left in a green car with a friend. Cindy or Mindy or something like that, " he said.

I said, "That doesn't make sense, Colt. I don't recall a friend named Cindy or Mindy. And why would she leave without her car? Can you return to Houston and help us look for her? You seem to be the last person to have seen her."

Colt responded, "That's not a good idea. Our engagement's over. It didn't end well."

I told him I had heard he had injured his hand, and I asked him how his hand was doing.

He replied, "It's okay. I cut it. I was opening a can of Vienna sausages. Look, I gotta go."

The conversation did not ring true. His explanations were inconsistent with what he'd told his grandmother, and they were in direct conflict with the note he'd left Wende. He never went to El Paso, never had a job lead in the area, and didn't give the same explanation about the cut on his hand. There was more to his story than he was sharing.

When we spoke to Wende's supervisor at Air Liquide, we learned that Wende had not reported to work on Thursday or Friday. They were concerned since this was not normal for her. We later learned, through witness statements from co-workers, that Wende had been complaining earlier in the week of sore ribs and a stomach ache. Did Colt have any part in this? Guess we'll never know unless Colt tells us.[3]

On Monday, the fourth of November, Wende's friends organized a search party in the neighborhood to look for any clues to her disappearance. They distributed flyers with her photo and description, walked the streets asking questions, and searched an adjacent drainage ditch. No trace of Wende.

Around nine thirty that same morning, the Constables' Office called and asked me to come to their neighborhood station. GG had already left for her real estate office, so

I went alone. Deputy Burke and Lieutenant Schwartz told me they had turned the investigation over to the Harris County Sheriff's Office in Houston because this was no longer a missing person's case, but rather a possible homicide. The Constables' Office did not have the experience or proper tools to investigate a homicide.

Meanwhile, that same day, my brother-in-law Mike and his wife Vanessa agreed to meet with Colt in an attempt to get him to help in the search for Wende. Mike was married to my sister, Marsha, until she died of breast cancer. Vanessa is his second wife. We are still close as requested by my sister. Mike and Vanessa had spent time with Colt and Wende in New Orleans and had a rapport with him. Mike picked up Colt for breakfast the next morning, the fifth of November, at the friend's house in Palestine, Texas. Colt told him he and Wende had had a fight and she stabbed him in the hand.

Leaving a cell phone line open to Vanessa in case something went wrong, Mike drove Colt's car with Colt as the passenger. Mike tried to convince him to return to Houston. Colt asked instead that Mike drive him to his dad's house in Louisiana, but Mike refused. The meeting was a dead end, but at least we learned where Colt was keeping himself and that it didn't appear his car was involved in whatever had happened.

It was also on Tuesday, the fifth of November, that Detective Michael Ritchie of the Harris County Sheriff's Office was assigned as lead investigator for Wende's disappearance. Detective Ritchie had been a peace officer in Harris County for eight years. This would be his first case as lead detective.

Around four p.m. that day, I drove to Wende's house to meet Detective Ritchie and exchange contact information. Ritchie informed me that Wende's house was officially a crime scene and that a lot of work needed to be done to process it. He would need information from the forensic people, the Medical Examiner's Office, and much more data before they could make any determination as to what might have happened. Later that evening he called me with devastating news.

"I've got to tell you something that's not easy to say."

The forensic team had discovered so much blood evidence in the house on the walls, in the toilets, in the bedroom carpet, and especially in the bathtub that it was impossible for anyone to have lost that much blood and survived. Much later we learned from DNA testing that the blood was Wende's.

November fifth. The saddest day of my life. *Wende was dead.*

TWO

... WENDE

Remembering you is easy,
I do it every day.
Missing you is a heartache
That never goes away.
Paul Marshall

GOD BLESSED US IN the fall of 1969 with our second daughter, Wende. Had it been up to me, she would have been named Consuela, a beautiful Hispanic name. I suggested this to GG.

"Get a boat and call it *Consuela*," she said without hesitation.

End of discussion. So our daughter became Wende Gayle Marshall.

At about four months of age, we noticed that Wende had a wandering eye, a condition that needed correction as early as possible. I was in the Navy and stationed in San Diego at a time when the Navy had one of the world's preeminent eye doctors there. His services were

11

requested by the World Health Organization (WHO) to treat some of the most difficult eye problems around the globe. He started treating Wende and, after many months, gained her trust. This enabled him to take the finite measurements needed to do the corrective surgery. He repositioned the eye muscle so her eyes worked perfectly together. Psalm 103:6 says, "God makes everything come out right . . . ." As He often does, God stepped into our lives to bless us, and our daughter showed us that from even so young an age, she had come out a fighter.

Wende was a very attractive child who became a 5 foot 4 inch, slender young lady. She never seemed to gain weight, no matter what she ate. When she wanted to look beautiful, she could—a lesson learned from her mother, who taught both our daughters how to buy clothes that fit their personalities as well as their figures.

Wende was more adventurous than her older sister, Michele. I think of Wende as my hippie daughter and Michele as my princess. Wende loved to do things that challenged her! She was up for anything from skydiving to scuba diving, snow skiing to hiking, and to just about anything outdoors. And she loved to travel the world. She made trips to Mexico, Australia, Spain, Thailand, and Iraq. She exhibited much of my personality with her stubbornness and independence. She was Paul Marshall in a skirt. This was both a blessing and a curse as she was growing up.

For example, we always had trouble getting Wende to eat zucchini. One evening I drew the line. We were the adults. She was the child. She *would* eat the zucchini. We turned away for just a moment, and when we looked back, the zucchini was gone. Tough love paid off! Sometime later, our family was transferred to Houston. As we took apart the dining table, we found the petrified zucchini. So much for my hard-ass methods.

When she was a senior in high school, she had a tendency to cross the boundaries we set for her. In particular, she continually challenged our curfew rules. At one point, it became so bad we asked her to leave. She moved in with a friend. But within a week, stubborn me realized our home was incomplete without her. We were ready for her to move back home. I later learned that she and her mother spoke almost every day that she was gone. But from that ordeal she learned what rules triggered me to strict disciplinary action and modified her behavior accordingly.

She was also an animal lover, no matter what kind of animal. At about ten or eleven years old, she and her friend, Chris, helped our Golden Retriever deliver a litter of puppies while GG and I were away. She did fine until the afterbirth appeared. She and her sister adopted a pet rabbit, which they nurtured for six or seven years. She brought a stray cat home and tried to hide it from us, which, of course, was a total failure. So we adopted it. She mucked out horse stalls just to be near horses. She continued to demonstrate this love of animals until the day she was taken from us. We have her two rescue dogs living with us as a daily reminder of her loving kindness to all things big and small.

Wende went out of her way to help those in need whether four footed or two. That certainly was the case with several of her male friends who came from unhealthy and dysfunctional families. Wende had a compulsion to try to restore them. That effort wasn't very successful with Colt Morgan.

Although she was almost three years younger than her sister, Michele, they were very close. Wende took extra classes in school to try to catch up with her. She never quite managed it, but by high school she was only a year behind. This meant her college years began before she was mature enough to handle time away from home. She spent her freshman year in San Marcos at Southwest Texas State (LBJ's college). Partying there and in Austin was just too convenient. After a couple of semesters, we had her move back home to take classes at a local junior college. She needed to get her priorities straight.

She did well in junior college and eventually headed off to Stephen F. Austin in Nacogdoches, Texas. We were very proud and excited. But when we attended graduation, her college folder held no diploma. She was three hours short of a B.A. This was a surprise to her, too. It wasn't until six years later that she was able to gain her degree through a correspondence course. Why the lapse in time only Wende knew for certain.

After graduation, Wende started working for a title company doing title searches. This was before electronic filing, so she had to locate paper files and research by title company, a very tedious process. After a year of struggling financially on $10 an hour, we suggested she move back home and work as her mother's assistant in residential real estate. We thought she was doing well, but apparently Wende did not feel the same. She decided she had a better idea for making money—transporting cocaine into Australia.

It is unclear what role her new boyfriend, John, had in this plan, but many of her cousins are convinced that he was the instigator. Wende enlisted the help of her best friend, Jenn, to carry out this scheme. They hollowed out tennis shoes and created waist bands to conceal the low-grade cocaine. Apparently, they were set up as a distraction from the transport of a higher grade of the drug. They were immediately apprehended upon landing in Sydney. As far as we knew, she was surfing in Mexico with John. This all changed when we received a call from Sydney at two a.m. informing us of her arrest.

Her first visitors in jail were Salvation Army Officers, Majors Joyce and Hilton Harmer. Having been raised by Salvation Army Officers myself, this was a special blessing to me! Their motto of "Heart to God — Hand to man" has been a mantra for me throughout my life. It was growing up in the Salvation Army that taught me that there is always hope and forgiveness for whatever bad decisions someone makes in their life. God is wonderful in how He provides for us when we most need it. While the commute from Houston to Sydney for prison visits was a trial, GG, Michele, and I managed it several times with assistance from the Harmers in finding lodging for us.

The Australian criminal system is fashioned more after the British system than the U.S. system. It took us a while to get used to the wigs, judges, lawyers, and solicitors. Together, we and Jennifer's family interviewed and selected a team to represent our daughters at trial. But the judge did not allow both girls to be represented by the same legal team, so Jennifer's parents selected a different lawyer. Wende received a forty-month sentence because she purchased the airline tickets and was considered the leader. Jennifer got thirty-six months.

We quickly learned much more about the Australian prison system and the many ways in which it differs from the U.S. system. For instance, women prisoners are required to perform jobs upon incarceration. Because Wende had four years of college and Jennifer was an office manager, they usually had pretty good jobs. At that time, I was an independent consultant, and one of my major clients was an Australian Engineering and Construction Company. I was working with the CEO, and he generously agreed to hire Wende as an Executive Assistant. She was allowed to work during the business week, but she had to return to the prison every night. Again, God stepped in and assisted us during this very difficult time in our lives.

Another benefit of the Australian prison system was KAIROS. KAIROS is a Christian faith-based support group for families with loved ones in prison. While involved with KAIROS, Wende was allowed to go on a weekend retreat with GG and Michele. We consider her KAIROS friends to have been angels in the Australian courtroom. She was soon moved to a Trustee position.

When Wende came back from Australia and her time with KAIROS, she had a different attitude. She became more active in the lives of people she knew, and she appeared to be much more appreciative of who she was, what she had, and the love and support of her family and friends. Many of the women in the Australian prison system had none or very little of that in their life experiences. KAIROS taught Wende more about Christianity than anything we had exposed her to in her childhood, possibly because she was more ready to listen while incarcerated. She came home with a better head for decisions, especially for being able to see actions and their consequences.

Wende had a variety of jobs before she finally found a niche she seemed to enjoy: Contract Management and Administration. After spending almost three years working in Iraq with Contracts Management, Wende came home with enough money to buy a house. She bought a modest three bedroom two bath home with a fireplace and a nice yard where she planted a garden. Best of all, it was close to her friend Jenn. One of my most treasured possessions is the closing paper on Wende's house where the new owner is Wende G. Marshall, the real estate agent is her mother, GG Marshall, and the loan officer is her sister, Michele.

Wende had several friends who were boys (but not necessarily *boyfriends*) that stayed at her house after she returned from Australia. Some paid rent or provided some sort of work in kind, like cutting the grass, taking out the garbage, and changing the oil in her car. Wende was in her home for more than three years when Colt moved in. Knowing Wende, the same kind of work for lodging arrangement was expected of Colt. Possibly his lack of meeting this expectation was a factor in the argument that led to her murder.

THREE

OH MY GOD!
HOW DO WE PROCESS THAT?

*Up to that point we had some hope
that we'd find Wende alive.*
PAUL MARSHALL

IN OUR MEETING ON the fifth of November, we told Detective Ritchie about the strange conversation we'd had with Colt on the evening of Sunday, the third of November. Ritchie used our information to call Colt at his friend's number in Palestine.

After careful review of the crime scene, Detective Ritchie called to tell us the Sheriff's Office didn't think Wende's body ever left the house. The Homicide Team believed that Colt repeatedly stabbed Wende and watched as she bled out and died. It appeared to them that he then butchered her body and burned her remains in her fireplace in a failed attempt to cover up the murder.

Oh my God! How do we process that? Up to that point, we had some hope that we'd find Wende alive. We now knew

Colt had murdered Wende, but with very little physical evidence, Detective Ritchie said it would be unlikely he could obtain an arrest warrant. There was no physical evidence linking Colt to the murder.

On the sixth of November, Detective Ritchie visited Colt at his friend's house in Palestine, identifying Colt with a booking photo from the Harris County Sheriff's Office database. In the interview, Colt admitted the cut was from a kitchen knife. He said Wende stabbed his hand with the knife, and he back-handed her, causing a bloody nose. Blood from her nose sprayed the walls. He ran into the bathroom to clean his wounded hand. While it was clear to Detective Ritchie that the amount of blood on the walls and carpet padding, as well as the bathtub, was far more than could be produced by Colt's description of the injuries, Colt maintained this version of events. Detective Ritchie observed the wound on Colt's right hand appeared to be a slicing type wound rather than a stabbing wound. Colt insisted he hadn't seen Wende since Halloween.[1]

The next morning, Detective Ritchie called to say he needed a DNA sample from me. He met me at my home to take a cheek swab. Later that morning he asked for one from GG to check mitochondrial DNA. This would only be available from Wende's mother. DNA results would not be available for several months, so they would not be of much use for issuing an arrest warrant, but they might eventually be needed as evidence at trial.

After the interview, Detective Ritchie confiscated Colt's car to search for evidence but found none. Sometime after this meeting, Colt's Palestine friend asked him to leave.

Apparently, he'd become uncomfortable with the investigation into Colt as well as the searches on his property. From there, Colt disappeared for a few weeks into local, remote, wooded areas where temperatures in November were in the range of 35 to 40 degrees Fahrenheit. However, there were hunting cabins and other uninhabited lodgings in the area, so he had opportunities for foraging,[2] and law enforcement found evidence of tarps and lean-tos.[3] Eventually, the conditions forced him to move to more inhabited locations like Buffalo, Texas.

Buffalo is a small Texas town in Leon County about an hour or so south of Dallas on I-45. Not accustomed to a lot of crime, its police department in 2013 consisted of only five full time officers led by Chief Lance Pavelka. Colt was breaking into homes and stealing weapons, food, cash, and clothing. His activities terrorized the residents in this area. Law enforcement eventually found evidence of makeshift shelters made with garbage bags and duct tape where Colt must have stayed during his time there. On the twenty second of November, Buffalo PD received a burglary call. A four-wheeler, a Glock handgun, and cold weather gear were missing.[4,5]

The house break-ins and criminal activity set the stage for an encounter with one of Buffalo's police officers on the twenty third of November. Officer Steven Pate found Colt in the parking lot of a local convenience store searching through a garbage can.

"I'm just going to check you for weapons," he told Colt, who at first appeared to be calm but then tried to pull out a pistol concealed in his waistband. He head-butted the officer and was hit by a taser. The taser forced him to the ground, but one of the prongs was dislodged. Colt escaped, but not before dropping the Glock .40 caliber pistol. As a result of this assault on a police officer, his bond was raised from $60,000 to $250,000 in Harris County.[6,7,8,9]

The broadcast of the police dash cam showing the head-butting kept the story alive.

The next day, the Buffalo Police Department held a press conference. They announced a coordinated manhunt with statewide law enforcement agencies including the U. S. Marshals, Texas Department of Public Safety, the Leon County Sheriff's Office, Texas Department of Criminal Justice, and the Texas Rangers. As part of this effort, they distributed flyers and posters around Leon County. After two weeks and no new sightings, the manhunt stalled.[10]

By December 3, 2013, Colt's trail had gone cold for the detectives in Houston. Leads had almost ceased, so I decided to grant an interview with Tiffany Craig of Channel 11 in Houston. Many news reporters had approached me for interviews, but I'd been advised by several respected voices, especially the attorney from the District Attorney's Office on Wende's case, to stay away from them out of fear that what I said could be used by Colt's defense team. Yet I was determined that we needed the public's help to find and capture Colt. We had no idea where he was, and he was still very capable of deadly harm to anyone in his way. GG had nightmares about him returning to Houston and attempting to harm us.

Tiffany Craig and I spoke about how heartbroken we were

about Wende and about our concern for the people in East Texas with Colt still at large. She allowed me to say what I wanted to say without much editing or coaching. Between the police encounter in Buffalo and the Tiffany Craig interview, Colt became headline news again.

On the tenth of December, a maintenance worker named Adrian, who worked for several Buffalo area motels, recognized Colt sleeping in a maintenance shed near the Buffalo Hampton Inn.[11]

"I unlocked the door, and I saw so much stuff that wasn't mine," Adrian told a KBTX reporter. "I had seen his face on the news." His call to the Buffalo Police awakened Colt. Startled, he ran into the woods, leaving behind all his personal items. After a short chase, Officers Rigo Mata and Josh Jordan of the Buffalo Police caught him on a back road.

"At first he wouldn't stop, but then he got on his knees, and he nonchalantly acted like he hadn't done anything wrong," said Chief Pavelka to KBTX.

Inside the shed, they found his backpack, a rifle, a pistol, and evidence that he was trying to make a silencer out of a plastic coke bottle, all left behind in his haste to run. "There was a lot of quarters, change, a .22 rifle, medication for horses," Chief Pavelka reported to KBTX.[12,13,14,15]

Colt was transferred to Palestine to await his return to Houston since Buffalo didn't have a jail.

The next day, Detective Ritchie drove to Palestine to take Colt into custody. Detective Ritchie told me I'd be the first one he contacted once Colt was caught. He wanted me to hear him slap the handcuffs on Colt before he put him in the car and drove him to Houston. Unfortunately, that didn't happen because I was driving to Atlanta to transfer ownership of Wende's car to GG's sister. Frustrating all around! But Colt had been apprehended and was no longer a danger to the general public.

Colt was physically exhausted and hungry. Detective Ritchie interviewed him at the Palestine Police Department.

"Wende assaulted *me*. I was just protecting myself. She had issues," Colt told Ritchie. "She killed herself. I did what I did."[16,17]

On the drive back to Harris County, Colt offered to confess if given some food. The Sheriff's Detectives exited the interstate and turned into the first fast food place they could find. It was a Wendy's. After feeding him, Colt admitted his crime. Yet he insisted that it was self-defense.

The interview ended.

When they arrived in Houston, Ritchie got a more detailed confession from Colt in a formal interrogation. Colt admitted to murdering Wende. He and Wende had been arguing, and he grabbed a knife. That one impulsive action began a horrific chain of events that devastated two families who loved their children—the Marshalls and Colt's mother, brother, and grandmother.

Colt was in the Harris County Jail. Now all we had to do was wait. And wait. And wait.

FOUR

*The Marshall family received a painful education in the
Criminal Justice System in the State of Texas.*
PAUL MARSHALL

FROM THE TIME OF his capture in December
2013, Colt was incarcerated in the Harris County Jail in
Houston until his court dates were finalized. The jail was
overcrowded and understaffed, and it was certainly not
a place anyone would desire to be. Many of our friends
thought Colt got what he deserved, but it wasn't anything
our family wanted for him. We were just anxious either
to get on with the trial or to obtain a guilty plea so he
could begin his prison sentence. Thus, we started a long
and painful hurry-up-and-wait period, looking for some
closure on this horrific tragedy.

Some of the things uncovered during this period revolved
around the inconveniences of trying to tie up the loose
ends of a person's life, especially when it happens so unex-
pectedly. We were unsuccessful in locating Wende's will.
We also learned through credit card bills that she had been
living beyond her means in support of Colt since he was
unemployed at the time of her murder. Many of the credit

card companies wrote off the charges when they heard about Wende's murder. Some had seen national news coverage about the violence done to her and expressed sympathy. Others insisted on payment. I usually negotiated a settlement with these companies. Only two credit card companies insisted on full payment. I quit discussing settlement options and eventually heard nothing more from them.

The Marshall family received a painful education in the Criminal Justice System in the State of Texas. *Swift justice* is a myth. There were constant delays either by the overworked court-appointed defense attorney or the judge. The prosecuting attorneys from the District Attorney's Office changed several times, requiring additional delays in preparing for trial. It took almost three years to get a firm trial date. According to Detective Ritchie, this was a typical time frame for this type of case.[1]

In preparing for the trial, we were asked to visit with the two prosecuting attorneys on several different occasions. What we learned about Colt during that time—his criminal history and his violence against our daughter—was particularly disturbing. It was during one of those visits that I was allowed to review most of the forensic evidence. It sickened me to the point that I knew my family and Wende's closest friends would not be able to handle the evidence displayed at trial.

Colt Morgan had a criminal history. According to Colt's TDCJ Criminal History, he'd received a two-year sentence for burglary of a habitation in Montgomery County, Texas, in 2010.[2] According to a KHOU11 news article, Colt Morgan also had a DWI conviction in 2012 in Gonzales County as well as previous convictions for drug possession, burglary, and theft dating back to 2005.[3]

Then we heard the gruesome discoveries of the forensic team upon examination of Wende's home.

Pursuant to a search warrant dated November 5, 2013, the forensic team found large quantities of blood spatter using luminol[4] and an alternate light source specifically for viewing cleaned blood stains. The blood was most concentrated in the doorway of the master bedroom and the tub in the hall bath. Human hair was clumped on the back side of the master bedroom door with more blood spatter on top of it. The crude paint job was only on top of the blood stains and not on the surrounding wall. Remains of a scrubbing pad were in the fireplace, and a number of towels were in the washing machine, post wash cycle. The team found fragments of human bone outside the home in the flowerbed and on the fence. Gardening tools, including a hoe, a pickaxe, a rake, and a post hole digger, had burned residue on them similar to what one would find when burning fat to a metal tool over an open flame. When the forensic anthropologist, Dr Jennifer Love, examined the scene on November 7 and 8, 2013, she identified pieces of human bone in the fireplace including fragments of finger, toe, ankle, skull, and rib bone—all badly burned. Outside in the garden, they found more human remains including a piece of a human skull.[5,6]

On Halloween night, Wende's neighbors in her Cypress suburb of Bonaire had noticed thick black smoke all night long coming from her chimney. They described an awful smell like burning plastic that lingered for a couple of days.[7]

It was so difficult to comprehend something so barbaric, so brutal, and so inhuman as this evidence, especially happening to someone you love so deeply as we loved Wende. Then I remembered Proverbs 3:5. "Trust in the Lord with all your heart and lean not on your own understanding." And I knew He would see me through this.

I also learned that this crime, as brutal and violent as it was, did not constitute capital murder, so the death penalty did not apply. And Colt had recanted his confession, claiming that it was given under duress. Instead, he said Wende's death had occurred while he was defending himself. The DA's Office felt that a life sentence was possible due to the nature of the murder, but there were no guarantees in a jury trial. We learned that a life sentence was about equal to a fifty-year sentence in the eyes of the court.

Prosecutors were excellent in offering us advice and recommendations regarding court proceedings, jury trials, and the evidence they possessed. They assisted us as we evaluated a jury trial where Wende would be vilified and dragged through the mud and where forensic evidence would be very graphic and highly disturbing to our family and Wende's friends. They warned us of the unpredictable nature of a jury trial. In the end, they were able to help us arrive at a plea bargain we were willing to accept.

At this point, the family just wanted some closure without exposing family and friends to all the painful and graphic evidence. Through several meetings between Colt's attorney, Anthony Osso, and the Harris County DA's Office, Colt agreed to a forty-year sentence. As part of the plea agreement, Leon County dropped its assault of a public servant charges against Colt.[8]

On Tuesday, March 8, 2016, Colt Morgan pleaded guilty to Wende's murder in the 184th District Court in Harris County, so the Marshall family was spared the torment of reliving the horrific ordeal through a trial.[8,9] I believe we have Colt's mother, Teresa, to thank for that. Colt admitted, through his attorney, to arguing with Wende in her home, to stabbing and killing her, attempting to burn her body in her fireplace, and burying what was left in the backyard. Originally, we thought he had dismembered her body, but in his confession he explained that he'd folded her into a fetal position and crammed her into the fireplace.[10]

Our family and Wende's friends took up two rows of seats in the Harris County courtroom. Eventually, we were given time to address Colt and the Court prior to sentencing. I was carrying Wende's cremation urn in my hands as well as a large picture of Wende when I addressed him. He looked me in the eyes as I spoke.

"You murdering, burning, butchering bastard. By killing Wende in so brutal a fashion, you betrayed a woman who loved you and tried to help you get your life back together. Your senseless and barbaric murder of our daughter will never dim our memories of Wende."

GG also addressed Colt. She was far more articulate than I, and Colt was not able to look directly at her. She pointedly reminded him of the years he had ahead of him to think about his actions.

The Honorable Jan Crocker sentenced Colt Morgan to forty years in the Texas Department of Corrections in a prison in Huntsville, Texas. Because of overcrowding in the prison system, he will be eligible for parole after serving half of that time in 2033. We have been told by many in the Criminal Justice System that due to the nature of his crime, Colt will not be granted a parole hearing after 20 years, but many things could happen to change that situation before 2033.

Does it really matter if Colt is paroled in 2033 or later? GG and I will likely no longer be around at that time. But unless Colt makes a dramatic change in his life, he still represents a danger to society. Wende's sister, Michele, will still be around and will have to live through the turmoil of a parole hearing. Detective Ritchie has assured me, however, that he will be at that parole hearing and speaking as a voice for Wende even if GG and I are gone.[11]

I have some final words on working with law enforcement.

1. Establishing trust and respect helped us relate to the homicide team.
2. Sharing all our thoughts, even when they seemed insignificant, was important to the investigation, possibly providing a missing piece they needed.
3. The hardest part for us was knowing when to ask questions without interfering.
4. We had to be patient! Building a case that would stand up in court and get a guilty verdict was going to take some time.

Philippians 4:13 assures me that I can do all things through

Christ who strengthens me. Working through closure and forgiveness would test that assurance as would the years before my family would have to relive this nightmare at a parole hearing. With my statement to Colt on March 8, 2016, the process of working through this forgiveness had just begun.

GG and Paul Marshall.

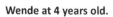

Wende at 4 years old.

Cheerleader at Pine Hollow Junior High School.

Wende relaxing with sister Michele, circa 1993.

Wende with Michele at Michele's wedding in 2011.

Wende on her birthday.

Prom night.

FIVE

It is one of the greatest gifts you can give yourself,
to forgive.
— MAYA ANGELOU

THERE IS A SPARK of goodness in everyone. How do
we reach it? We can't without God's help. This is where
our faith, our family, and our friends played a significant
role in helping us retain our sanity. It was our family and
friends who inspired us to rely on God to get us through
this. But this forgiveness did not happen for me overnight.
Forgiveness, at least in my case, was a series of small steps,
starting with focusing on beautiful and wonderful memories of Wende, such as listening to Wende and her mother
discussing new recipes or the simple pleasure of hearing
my two daughters laughing together.

When Wende was in Thailand, I asked her to bring back
precious stones that I could have made into jewelry for the
three women in my family. She brought back opals and
rubies. I took the gems to Jami Taylor who designed some
beautiful bracelets, necklaces, and earrings from them. The
fire opals, which are a soft white stone with reddish high-
lights, are particularly stunning. More important to me

than the jewelry, though, is the memory of the one who was so considerate of my request. She went out of her way to get what I asked for.

Neither of our daughters ever hesitated inviting us to their social functions. I remember watching a Super Bowl at a place called the Thirsty Texan in a crowd of young people. There was raucous behavior all around us, but the girls felt comfortable with us in any kind of setting.

Through all of this, God brought me to many *what am I supposed to learn from this?* moments. It is being a Jesus follower—reading daily devotionals, praying many times each day, reading God's Word—that has brought me to forgiveness. Sharing my pain and suffering with my loving family and friends has eased and expedited the process for me.

All of my life I have been taught that the only way through tragedy is forgiveness in all circumstances, no matter how terrible or difficult. It is an absolute necessity in order to move forward. But forgiveness is almost impossible for me without a strong belief in Jesus. His life is an example of what forgiveness is all about. He forgave the thief hanging beside Him as well as those who put Him there. "Father, forgive them for they know not what they do" (Luke 23:34). Forgiveness is not simply forgetting the offense or the absence of pain. Neither is it cancelling the tragedy or receiving an explanation of *why*. Instead, it is an act of obedience to God and a reflection of what Jesus has done for me.

The three years of investigation and trial preparation took my mind away from considering forgiveness. We initially thought we'd find a body. The truth was grotesque and cruel, leaving us in shock. How could we deal with this? GG believes that the first stab killed Wende instantly. I believe he watched her bleed out. It is difficult to conceive of the rage that drove Colt to do this. I felt intense anger toward Colt and the court system for a long time. It wasn't until I could face Colt in the courtroom that my healing began.

Forgiveness is a complex process and everyone approaches it at their own pace. It is a culmination of steps moving away from wanting revenge and questioning God to accepting that there is evil in the world, but God is still in control. Sometimes I felt like I made giant steps toward forgiveness for no apparent reason and other times it was like I was moving backwards for no apparent reason. But I eventually moved on to the realization that without forgiveness, Wende's tragedy would continue to control me in some fashion forever.

I learned from a program called GriefShare that we all grieve in a different way. I feel strong pangs of regret that I will never have a grandchild. Part of my grief expressed itself in anger with God about this. Fortunately, I know He is big enough to take it and still love me.

GG has told me her chief regret is that Wende never reached her full potential, having spent so much time floundering to find her niche in life. She seemed to have found it in working with people and solving contract service issues. She was on the brink of making it her career. GG's approach to forgiveness is somewhat different than mine. She has turned Colt over to God. He, and He alone, knows His plan for Colt's life. I feel called by the Holy

Spirit to take a more active role in achieving forgiveness. This is my primary reason for writing this book.

One of the things about Wende that always stood out to me was how ready she was to forgive people. This aspect of her character is an inspiration to me. Her kindness toward both people and animals always reminds me of how loving she was. Her two beloved rescue dogs, Tori and Terra, are living with GG and me as another poignant reminder of her absence. They are so loving and gentle, and it pains me that she is not here to take care of them. If she can show love and forgiveness toward others, I need to love and forgive as well.

I grew up watching my parents, as Salvation Army Officers, work with people who had made some truly bad decisions in their lives. I witnessed firsthand how God worked through forgiveness for some pitiful life stories. We were living on the Big Island of Hawai'i when refugee Salvation Army Officers from Korea shared their stories of misery and heartache that were bred in that conflict. Their example of forgiveness for the actions of the North Korean invasion of South Korea was an early reminder of the need to forgive. I also heard how even those considered the enemy gave them aid. Certainly the South Koreans sheltered them as they fled the war-ravaged areas of the country, but they also told stories of North Korean Christians providing them security and safety until they were evacuated.

I was a Division Officer in the Navy in the Vietnam years and responsible for the command of many young men. About 60 percent of them were under 19 years of age. Some of them joined the Navy because a judge gave them a choice of Vietnam or prison. Some of these individuals were from opposing gangs and required regular governance to work through personal as well as interpersonal problems.

One young man was the leader of a Black street gang in Chicago. He was a natural born leader. This was back in the early 1970s when Black and White gang wars were particularly violent. On one occasion, this young gang leader from Chicago was ambushed in one of the hallways at about one or two a.m. He and his assailant beat the crap out of each other. I arranged a meeting with the leader of the White gang and the leader of the Black gang. I and my other officers—the Chief Aviation Bosun who was responsible for crash salvage operations and all accidents on the ship plus the Chief Warrant Officer who was the senior enlisted officer—took the ranks off our collars. Effectively, each of us took off our officer mask. We made it clear to them that they needed to clean up this situation or someone was going to end up dead.

The offenders were sent to the brig, which was run by Marines. It meant thirty days of bread and water. The Black leader got himself squared away after this and eventually was promoted to "Yellow Shirt," a flight deck leader, a highly esteemed accomplishment. This experience made me realize that each of us needs forgiveness for things we have done.

Our Christian body of faith, Windwood Presbyterian Church, arranged a beautiful memorial service for Wende. Some of the adult members of this church attended childhood Sunday School classes with her and always mention her when we run into each other Sunday mornings. The sanctuary, which holds about 400, was overflowing with people gathered to celebrate Wende's life. This turnout occurred even though we never published an obituary column for Wende out of concern that Colt was still at large. GG and I spent more than an hour greeting and thanking people for their attendance. Many members of the Chancel Choir attended and sang "Give Me Jesus" as part of the celebration of Wende's life. We were blessed by the tributes delivered by her friends. I had the honor of representing the Marshall family with a eulogy to the wonderful impact Wende had on our lives. I spoke about how lucky we were that God had shared her with us for forty-four years. Allowing bitterness and anger to destroy those memories would have been tragic. Failing to forgive the offending party means he still has a hold on you. Forgive him, and you set the prisoner—yourself—free!

I also received support from a group that meets at First Presbyterian Church in Houston called *Parents of Murdered Children*. They went into detail concerning what to expect with the Texas Justice System, warning that Colt's only defense would be to paint Wende as dirt. They also encouraged me not to let the defense attorney push us around. We went through six court date delays at the insistence of Colt's defense attorney.

It was several weeks after Wende's murder before Detective Ritchie called to let us know the forensic team had processed Wende's remains. They were available for pick up. We made arrangements with a crematorium in Conroe, Texas, to prepare her remains. Normally the cremains of a human body weigh between six and eight pounds.

Wende's weighed fourteen ounces. Colt almost succeeded in completely destroying Wende's 110-pound body.

We placed Wende's cremains in a beautifully lacquered Thailand jewelry box that she'd brought back from one of her international trips. This box was then placed in a columbarium at Windwood Presbyterian Church where we had a second memorial service for her with wonderful music, beautiful reassuring words of faith, and the assurance of God's promise of Wende's place in heaven where we will eventually join her. A large release of balloons with hand written notes of love and prayers from her many friends followed the service. This balloon release did not go off exactly as planned. I had ordered 100 helium-filled balloons the day before the service, but the order had not been filled by the time I arrived that day. The entire store went into General Quarters to try to fill my order, but time ran out at about 50 balloons. Yet this worked out even better than planned, because it meant asking people to share balloons. People who did not know each other were drawn together sharing memories of Wende. It was an extremely moving day for the Marshall family, and it brought some partial closure to the entire tragedy.

I do not know God's plan for Colt, but I pray that Colt hears God's call while incarcerated. There are many wonderful faith-based programs in the TDCJ that could alter Colt's outlook on life. It is our hope and prayer that he takes advantage of opportunities to repent of his actions.

The Heart of Texas Foundation is one such program. This foundation offers a course of study leading to a BA in Theology. Graduates from the prison system are assigned to different prisons to start small worship groups. They live in the cells with the other prisoners, do all the required duties of a prisoner, and are strongly encouraged to form individual churches to bring other prisoners to Christ. This program has produced wonderful results in reducing crime and violence in the Texas Department of Criminal Justice (TDCJ) and Louisiana prison systems.

If I had the opportunity to address Colt Morgan today, I would tell him I hope he has finally come to the realization that he, and he alone, is responsible for this tragedy and that with his actions he hurt so many people, both Wende's family and friends as well as his own family. I hope he has learned to tame his use of drugs and alcohol and that he goes to God with true repentance for his sins through Christ. My hope for him is that he finds a Christian study and worship group in prison and that he learns a trade so he can support himself when he is released. Finally, I want him to know that we have forgiven him, but we can never forget what he did to our family.

As far as our own lives are concerned, we have no firm idea of God's plans, but I feel called to share this experience with anyone who will listen. God tells us through the prophet Jeremiah: "For I know the plans I have for you says the LORD. They are plans for good and not for evil to give you a future" (Jeremiah 29:11). You will never get to the *good* without forgiveness.

I have come to peace with the murder, but not an understanding of it. I can't say that I fully comprehend what God wants me to learn from all of this, but I accept that it is possible this was also about Him reaching out to Colt with our family playing a role in his salvation. It's not that I think God wanted any of this to happen, but rather that He can use even the most horrific circumstances to bring about something good. It has taken a lot of prayer and patience, but I think I have finally come to a place of acceptance. While I still hurt when I hear the song "Wendy," and anger against Colt wells up inside, each time it is more diminished. I don't think it will ever go away entirely.

To anyone who has suffered wrong at the hand of others and continues to harbor anger, I pray that you come to realize that while the hurt and pain will never go away, you must forgive others as Jesus has forgiven you and move on or it will cripple your life. Lean on God and on the strong support of your family and friends. Together, they will get you through the tragedies in your life.

ACKNOWLEDGMENTS

. . . a cord of three strands is not easily broken.
ECCLESIASTES 4:12 HCSB

MANY HEARTFELT THANKS ARE in order for all of the professionalism, compassion, and love shared with our family throughout this ordeal.

The particularly horrific way in which Wende was murdered supplied a special motivation to the **Harris County Sheriff's Office detective team, including Michael Ritchie, David Angstadt, Sgt. Spurgeon, Frank Garcia, and Chris Cooke**.

I felt a strong connection with **Detective Michael Ritchie**. He seemed to know when to provide us an update, and we always felt he kept us adequately informed about the status of the investigation and what next steps were needed to issue an arrest warrant on Colt. GG was especially appreciative that the team always referred to Wende by her name and not as *the victim*. Andrew, my son-in-law, was particularly impressed that law enforcement helicopters circled the crime scene and the CyFair Volunteer Fire Department had their high-powered lights shining on

Wende's property when the HCSO team, led by Detective Ritchie, presented themselves as a show of force on the scene. The team did an outstanding professional job, respecting our need for privacy while also keeping us informed as events dictated. We were privileged to recognize them in a meeting with Michael's boss, the Harris County Sheriff.

The prompt action by the **Harris County Precinct 4 Constables** to declare Wende's case a possible homicide and hand it to the Harris County Sheriff's Office assisted a great deal in a situation where time was critical. Kudos to **Precinct 4 Constables Joel Burke and Lt. Schultz**.

The circle of **Wende's friends** who posted flyers, sent out emails, and went on a door-to-door search after Wende's disappearance displayed an amazing demonstration of love and respect. After learning of Wende's murder, they gathered all of her personal items and brought them to us. They sold the remaining effects—furniture, kitchenware, tools, and clothing—on eBay or at garage sales. This was a close-knit group of women, and we are grateful for their efforts.

I was pleased to have the opportunity to visit with **Adrian**, the hotel worker in Buffalo who reported finding Colt hiding out in a maintenance shed. With the help of Crime Stoppers, he was rewarded for being a responsible citizen in reporting Colt's location.

I also had the opportunity to meet the **Buffalo police officers** responsible for Colt's capture and thank them for their participation in bringing Colt to justice.

I have never met **Colt's mother, Teresa,** but we owe her a great deal for her assistance in providing us insights about Colt and informing us of contact numbers to reach him as well as her role in achieving a plea bargain. Who knows where we would have been in the investigation without her help? My family thanks her and appreciates how she has stayed in contact with us. We know that she and her family have been devastated by all of this too.

We could not have gotten through this emotionally without the love and guidance from—

1. The **Parents of Murdered Children,** a support group with parents whose children have never been found. They taught me that there are others far worse off than I.
2. Our family of faith, **Windwood Presbyterian Church,** for all of its personal support and spiritual strength, especially to the men of the Man to Man group and their many hours of listening.
3. The **U.S. Naval Academy Alumni Class of 1965** for their presence at Wende's memorial service in a much-appreciated show of emotional support.
4. **GriefShare** for its personal guidance through the grieving process.

Finally, we give thanks to **God** who is the source of all hope, forgiveness, and love.

Paul Marshall
January 2022

SOURCES

ONE

1. Morgan, Colt. Note to Wende Marshall. 31 Oct 2013. MS. Harris County Sheriff's Office Property Room 601 Lockwood, Houston.

2. Ritchie, M.A.. Harris County Sheriff's Office. *Incident Report 13-152558 Supplement No. 0010.* Houston: Office of Sheriff Ron Hickman, 11 Nov 2013. Print.

3. Cooke, C.J.. Harris County Sheriff's Office. *Incident Report 13-152558 Supplement No. 005.* Houston: Office of Sheriff Ron Hickman, 6 Nov 2013. Print.

THREE

1. Ritchie, M.A.. Harris County Sheriff's Office. *Incident Report 13-152558 Supplement No. 0010.* Houston: Office of Sheriff Ron Hickman, 11 Nov 2013. Print.

2. Ritchie, Michael. Personal Interview. 18 Oct 2021.

3. Smith, Victor. Leon County Sheriff's Office. *Leon County Sheriff's Office Time Line Fugitive Colt Morgan Manhunt.* Centerville: Leon County Sheriff's Office, n.d. Print.

4.   Ritchie, M.A.. Harris County Sheriff's Office. *Incident Report 13-152558 Supplement No. 0022.* Houston: Office of Sheriff Ron Hickman, 25 Nov 2013. Print.

5.   Smith, Victor. Leon County Sheriff's Office. *Leon County Sheriff's Office Time Line Fugitive Colt Morgan Manhunt.* Centerville: Leon County Sheriff's Office, N.d.. Print.

6.   Smith, Victor. Leon County Sheriff's Office. *Incident Report 132490.* Centerville: Leon County Sheriff's Office Kevin Ellis, Sheriff, 10 Dec 2013. Print.

7.   Smith, Victor. Leon County Sheriff's Office. *Leon County Sheriff's Office Time Line Fugitive Colt Morgan Manhunt.* Centerville: Leon County Sheriff's Office, N.d.. Print.

8.   Ritchie, M.A.. Harris County Sheriff's Office. *Incident Report 13-152558 Supplement No. 0022.* Houston: Office of Sheriff Ron Hickman, 25 Nov 2013. Print.

9.   KBTX Staff. "Harris County Murder Suspect in Custody." (10 Dec 2013): n.page. KBTX.com. Web. Accessed 22 Dec 2018.

10. Smith, Victor. Leon County Sheriff's Office. *Leon County Sheriff's Office Time Line Fugitive Colt Morgan Manhunt.* Centerville: Leon County Sheriff's Office, N.d.. Print.

11. Palestine Herald Press Staff Reports. "Harris County murder suspect caught by Buffalo police Tuesday." (10 Dec 2013): n.page. palestineherald.com. Web. Accessed 22 Dec 2018.

12. KBTX Staff. "Harris County Murder Suspect in Custody." (10 Dec 2013): n.page. KBTX.com. Web. Accessed 22 Dec 2018.

13. Wilder, Susan. "Colt Morgan Sentenced to 40 Years." (15 Mar 2016): n.page. buffaloexpressnews.com. Web. Accessed 22 Dec 2018.

14. Sallee, Wayne. Leon County Sheriff's Office. *Event No. 13239 — Incident Report.* Centerville: Kevin Ellis, Sheriff, 3 Feb 2016. Print.

15. Palestine Herald Press Staff Reports. "Harris County murder suspect caught by Buffalo police Tuesday." (10 Dec 2013): n.page. palestineherald.com. Web. Accessed 22 Dec 2018.

16. Ritchie, M.A.. Harris County Sheriff's Office. *Incident Report 13-152558 Supplement No. 0023.* Houston: Office of Sheriff Ron Hickman, 25 Nov 2013. Print.

17. Ritchie, Michael. Personal Interview. 18 Oct 2021.

FOUR

1. Ritchie, Michael. Personal Interview. 18 Oct 2021.

2. TDJC Criminal History Colt D Morgan. The Texas Tribune, 2013, texastribune.org, Accessed 22 Dec 2018.

3. KHOU Staff and KHOU.com. "Man charged with murder in connection with death of girlfriend reported missing." (12 Nov 2013): n.page. KHOU.com. Web. Accessed 22 Dec 2018.

4. Ritchie, Michael. Personal Interview. 18 Oct 2021.

5. Ritchie, M.A.. Harris County Sheriff's Office. *Incident Report 13-152558 Supplement No. 0017.* Houston: Office of Sheriff Ron Hickman, 25 Nov 2013. Print.

6. Ritchie, M.A.. *State of Texas v. Colt D. Morgan Murder Arrest Warrant*. Harris County District Court No. 184. Houston: Harris County Clerk's Office, 8 Nov 2013. Print.

7. Ritchie, M.A.. Harris County Sheriff's Office. *Incident Report 13-152558 Supplement No. 0010*. Houston: Office of Sheriff Ron Hickman, 25 Nov 2013. Print.

8. Wilder, Susan. "Colt Morgan Sentenced to 40 Years." (15 Mar 2016): n.page. buffaloexpressnews.com. Web. Accessed 22 Dec 2018.

9. Spencer, Bill. "Man admits to brutal murder of fiancée." (8 Mar 2016): n.page. click2houston.com. Web. Accessed 22 Dec 2018.

10. Ritchie, M.A.. Harris County Sheriff's Office. *Incident Report 13-152558 Supplement No. 0022*. Houston: Office of Sheriff Ron Hickman, 25 Nov 2013. Print.

11. Ritchie, Michael. Personal Interview. 18 Oct 2021.

THOUGHT QUESTIONS

CHAPTER ONE

- How can you deal with the fear of uncertainty or fear of the worst in times of trial?

CHAPTER TWO

- Do you take the time to appreciate the strengths of loved ones (and others), especially when you might be dealing with their points of weakness or their frailties?

- Do you truly forgive and forget missteps in others, especially loved ones?

- Can you lean into faith in God in times of trial?

CHAPTER THREE

- When the tragedy of a situation overwhelms you, what sustains you?

- What helps you come to terms with wrongs done to you or your loved ones, especially if the wrong is far outside acceptable behavior?

CHAPTER FOUR

- Are we to be the judge of and proclaim that someone got what they deserved? Or didn't get what they deserved?

- How do you stop the memories of wrongs done from rekindling negative feelings, even thoughts of vengeance or retribution?

- How can you find a place to start your self-healing process when suffering from a wrong done to you or a loved one?

- Should there second chances for those who have done wrong? What guides this decision?

- If your perception of what would be "just" does not happen, how would this affect the way you deal with this wrong in your own healing?

CHAPTER FIVE

- Do you believe there is a spark of goodness in everyone? Why or why not?

- Can you fill your heart and mind with positive, loving memories and feelings to push away the dark?

About the Author

PAUL WAS BORN IN Lihue, Kauai, Hawaii. His parents were Salvation Army Officers serving the migrant workers in the sugar cane and pineapple fields. Growing up, Paul attended 11 different schools in 7 different cities since his family moved frequently for his parents' work. Later, Paul graduated from the U.S. Naval Academy, and then served three Aircraft Carrier tours in Vietnam, flying over 100 combat and combat support missions. He entered the Navy Reserves in 1975 and remained until his retirement in 1992 with the rank of Captain.

As a civilian, Paul worked in marketing and business development for major architect, engineering, and construction companies. His family's life was dramatically changed with the violent murder of his youngest daughter, Wende, by her fiancé.

He wrote this book to share the changes he went through from hatred and revenge to finally arriving at forgiveness. He says the journey was made possible by the absolute help of his strong Christian faith and the loving and caring of a devoted family and many loyal friends.

Today, Paul enjoys singing in the church choir, helping young people in their Christian walk, playing league tennis, and taking daily walks with the family's three adopted dogs, two of which belonged to Wende.

Made in the USA
Coppell, TX
15 November 2022

86425578R00036